COMRADE LAUGHTER

for Arnold Rattenbury

COMRADE
LAUGHTER

Andy Croft

FLAMBARD

Acknowledgements

The poet wishes to thank Arts Council England, North East for an Encore Award, which bought the time to work on this collection.

Versions of some of these poems first appeared in *Acumen, Evening Gazette, Moodswing, NALGAO News, The North, Penniless Press, Red Pepper, Sand* and *Thumbscrew*; in *For Arnold With Love*, ed. John Lucas, and *Smelter*, ed. Cynthia Fuller and Kevin Cadwallender; others have been broadcast on BBC Radio Cleveland, BBC 5 Live and BBC Radio 4; part of 'Letter to Randall Swingler Part II' appeared in *Authors Take Sides on Iraq*, ed. Jean Moorcroft Wilson and Cecil Woolf; 'Alchemical' was commissioned by the National Association of Local Government Arts Officers and written during their three-day conference in Newcastle in May 2002; 'Sunlight and Heat' was commissioned by Middlesbrough Borough Council to mark the 150th anniversary of the town's Charter of Incorporation in 2003; 'Why Aye, Minister' was commissioned for the London media-launch of Yes4theNorthEast at the Commonwealth Club in January 2004.

First published in the UK in 2004 by Flambard Press
Stable Cottage, East Fourstones, Hexham NE47 5DX
Typeset by BookType
Front-cover image: detail from 'Soldiers of the Future' by Ken Sprague
Cover design by Gainford Design Associates
Printed in England by Cromwell Press, Trowbridge, Wiltshire

A CIP catalogue for this book
is available from the British Library.
ISBN 1 873226 66 7

Flambard wishes to thank Arts Council England, North East
for its financial support.

website: www.flambardpress.co.uk

Contents

History is thorough and goes through many phases when carrying an old form to the grave. The last phase of a world-historical form is its *comedy*. The gods of Greece, already tragically wounded to death in Aeschylus's *Prometheus Bound*, had to die a comic death in Lucian's *Dialogues*. Why? So that humanity should part with its past cheerfully.

(Karl Marx)

A sense of humour is a splendid, healthy quality.

(Lenin)

I have never met anyone who could laugh so infectiously as Vladimir Ilyich.

(Maxim Gorky)

Good morning, Comrade Laughter,
There's plenty of work
For you here.

(Paul Potts)

Comrade Laughter

I think of you as short and fat,
A Chaplin–Chonkin–Svejk,
The little bloke who finds a joke
In what you most dislike,
And laughing at what you despise
Cuts down the mighty and the wise
   to size.

Except the joke's on us these days,
And History's in reverse:
The old regime is here to stay,
The jokes keep getting worse,
And if you think this means we're cheerful
I am afraid you risk a tearful
   earful.

Walking on Hampstead Heath with Adrian Mitchell

A brisk, post-breakfast walk, you said,
   Before I had to catch my train,
A little stroll to clear the head,
   Around the Heath and back again,

So we could talk of plays and books,
   Of poetry and politics,
While Daisy could go chasing ducks
   And tire you out with throwing sticks.

Along the way we stop to talk
   To friends and neighbours in the sun,
To poets and dogs out for a walk
   And dogs who make their poets run.

Before we know we've tagged along
   A crowd of yours and Daisy's chums,
Ten minutes more and we're a throng,
   A dogged host that soon becomes

An argument of tangled leads,
   Part Orpheus, part Dodie Smith,
A wagging tale of mongrel breeds
   And underdogs, a dog-eared myth

Of barking poets and talking dogs,
   Until we stand on Parliament Hill
And there below the lifting fogs
   Blake's London's waiting, shining still.

The Neon Thrush

I leant against the car-park wall
　　When frost was neon-pink,
Weighed down by bags of shopping full
　　Of New Year food and drink,
And tangled spools of tape uncurled
　　Among the car-park litter,
A silent soundtrack for a world
　　Grown old and cold and bitter.

The freezing car-park might have made
　　A fitting year's-end figure,
The word made skin and bones, clichéd
　　As Winter's iron rigor –
But all at once a voice arose
　　Among the shopping trolleys,
A song with which to juxtapose
　　The century's human follies.

Confused by car-park neon lights
　　To sing the coming dawn,
It sang instead the deathbed rites
　　Of vanities unborn.
False dawn, false start, O stupid bird!
　　An uninvited heckler,
Appropriate to this absurd
　　And gloomy *fin de siècle.*

A proper Y2K poseur!
　　As if to disregard
The deadened senses of the year
　　It sang this false aubade.
This night is like a two-faced dream,
　　The century's paradigm,
Where artless Nature can't redeem
　　What humans do in time.

31 December 2000

Dorotheenstädtischer Friedhof

'Once you've been beaten
What will remain?'
  (Bertolt Brecht)

Somewhere between the rebuilt tourist traps
  Of Checkpoint Charlie, bits of rubbled *Mauer*,
Potsdamer Platz, Red Army surplus shops,
  The plate-glass shrines to property and power,
Between the pavement icons of the poor,
  The lovers on the sunny streets of May,
The red-lights on Oranienburger Tor,
  The *Tränenpalast*'s tearful cabaret;
Between the Reichstag and the red Town Hall,
  Beneath the crane-built sky, the lilac blooms,
Behind Brecht's house, beyond a tree-hung wall,
  Between these grim sarcophagi and tombs,
Iron-gated crypts which hoard the last remains
  Of those who thought the grave a well-earned rest;
Among the great and good, the rich and vain,
  Who died believing death could be possessed;
Among three hundred years of Berlin dead,
  Professors, merchant bankers, architects,
Between the humble monuments to Reds
  Like Weigel, Eisler, Heartfield, Seghers, Brecht,
We almost miss this pansied, corner cairn
  Beneath the dusty, light-filled chestnut trees,
In memory of Liz Shaw, whose last remains
  Are now *bestattet* in the Irish Sea.
An overgrown and book-shaped little stone,
  It marks the place where art gives up its dead,
Where flesh and blood become just flesh and bone,
  The uncut page, the books we've never read;

Between the open book, the dreaming child,
  The copy that's remaindered and unsigned,
Between the hope that dies unreconciled,
  The journey and the life that's left behind;
Between the end of one world and the next,
  Between the exile and the homeless heart,
What must remain reads like the Spring's green text,
  A memory of patient love and art.

Dives and Lazarus

As it fell out upon a day
   Rich Dives he held a feast,
And he invited all his friends
   And gentry of the best.

They made themselves a national plan
   To better the nation's health,
And help themselves to the public purse
   To better their private wealth.

Then Lazarus laid him down and down
   And down at Dives' door,
'Some meat, some drink, brother Dives,
   Bestow upon the poor!'

But Dives was a busy man,
   And Dives locked his door,
For England is a friendless land
   If you are old and poor.

Then Dives sent his tabloid dogs
   To bite him as he lay,
And print their teeth marks on his flesh
   And hound him on his way.

And Dives sent his merry men
   To spin *The World at One*,
And lick his weeping sores until
   It seemed his sores were gone.

And Lazarus he was hungry,
   And Lazarus he was cold,
And Lazarus wasn't in BUPA
   So Lazarus he went cold.

And so it fell out upon a day
   Poor Lazarus sicken'd and died,
And Dives threw his corpse away
   Before his blood had dried.

And Lazarus he went straight to hell
   To burn for ever more,
For there is always the Devil to pay
   If you are sick and poor.

And it fell out upon a day
   That Dives sicken'd and died,
And Dives he went straight to heaven
   (Which now's been PFI'd).

For Dives was a rich man
   And rich men know what's theirs,
And when they've taken that they want
   To take the poor man's shares.

The rich will always feast and dine
   While others want for more;
Unless the poor throw off the rich
   The rich will keep them poor.

And public medicine will not thrive
   While there is private health,
And there'll be no cure for England's ills
   While there is private wealth.

Mudfog Declares War on Tourism

The Mayor of Mudfog said today
   He pledged his full support
To fight the Tourists all the way,
And would outlaw without delay
   Hawaiian shirt and shorts.

'No hiding place for Tourists here!'
   The Mayor of Mudfog cried,
'Our way of life will disappear,
The values that we most hold dear,
   If we just stand aside.'

The Tourist menace thus was met
   With Anti-Tourist laws,
To stop the foreign Tourist threat
And catch all those within the net
   Who live beyond these shores.

We started burning A–Zs
   And outlawed phrase-book phrases,
And burned the Tourists in their beds
And shot all those with crew-cut heads
   And sent them all to blazes.

We stopped the evil Tourist lot
   And shackled them in chains,
We smashed their cameras on the spot
To make quite sure that they would not
   Try Tourism again.

And now that they have run away
   And all the world is glad,
The Mayor of Mudfog left today
To start a five-week holiday
   In Kabul and Baghdad.

Kissinger to Head Investigation into September 11 Terror

'It makes no sense to issue some moral statement about democracy.'
(US State Department, 1 October 1973)

There are some dates that we should all remember
 Because they mark the day and place and time
When History – as on that fell September –
 Is terrorised by monsters in the slime,
When something so repulsive and primeval
 Crawls out to write its signature in blood,
And all the world is forced to watch as evil
 Devours the kind, the ordinary and good.

Remember then this date, because it led
 From Constitution Square to Pinochet
And 40,000-plus civilian dead,
 All planned and paid for by the USA.
It makes no sense, of course, except to men
Who've let the bloody monsters loose again.

Domino Effect

'There is nothing which can sharpen the historian's mind like defeat.'

(Eric Hobsbawm)

The pieces are all swept away
And sealed inside a wooden box
That's kept inside a metal chest
With bolts and combination locks
Beneath the cellar of a house
Abandoned since the stormy night
Tormented by the bottle's ghosts
The old man set himself alight
And burned it down upon the last
And missing pages of a book
That's stuck behind the driver's seat
Inside an ancient pick-up truck
That skids around a mountain bend
And hits a sudden fall of snow
Then plunges down a steep ravine
Exploding on the scree below
Just as the credits start to roll
And flicker in the final frame
In some re-run disaster dream
You've seen before but cannot name
In which the cinema's destroyed
By meteor, tidal wave and quake,
And though you try to hold your breath
You're drowning long before you wake
Inside a world of polished stone
As changeless as a dead lagoon
Beneath a silent mountain ridge
Somewhere on Pluto's furthest moon
Where nothing dies and nothing lives
And there's no after or before,
And nothing takes and nothing gives
And nothing matters any more.

Comrade Laughter at the End of the Pier

The jokers who now top the bill,
They really are a pair,
A priceless old-time music-hall
Routine called Blush and Bare.
If you could see them they would seem
The kind of double act you'd deem
    a scream.

Comrade Laughter Tries Stand-Up

There's these three politicians, right,
Called Blair and Bush and Straw,
They say that they are men of peace
Who hate the thought of war,
And though it's hard to fucking credit
It's true because they fucking said it.
    Geddit?

The Elephants of Mudfog

As the sun climbed up over the chimneys,
    And the traffic jams started to crawl,
Ten stone elephants marched into Mudfog
    And sat down beside the Town Hall.

Now nobody knew where they came from,
    Or what they were hoping to do,
Perhaps they'd escaped from a circus?
    Perhaps they belonged in a zoo?

A terrified crowd quickly gathered
    And stared at the marvellous sight,
Ten stone elephants sitting in Mudfog –
    It shouldn't be, couldn't be right!

Then someone alerted the council,
    Who called out the National Guard,
Who called for a SWAT team and air-strike,
    (Cos shooting an elephant's hard).

The elephants stared at the soldiers
    And blinked in the bright Mudfog sun,
Until a small child ran over and smiled
    And gave one a Greggs' currant bun.

The crowd watched in silent amazement
    As the elephant picked up the lad,
Then stood to its feet and walked down the street
    And brought him back safe to his dad.

Hurrah for the mammoths of Mudfog!
    Three cheers for our elephant chums!
Although it' s well known that they're just made of stone
    Their hearts are as big as their bums.

They soon were a local attraction,
    They even gave rides to the Mayor,
Folk came from afar, by coach and by car,
    To stare at them sat in the square.

They starred in a *Blue Peter* special,
    They handed out gongs at the Brits,
Took part in another new round of *Big Brother*,
    And modelled the new England kits;

There was talk of a remake of *Dumbo*,
    The National Lottery draw,
The rumours were thick of a *Hannibal* pic,
    A phone-in on Radio 4.

The jumbos were quite a sensation,
    They helped put the place on the map;
Some artists came down to visit the town
    In search of some elephant crap.

But alas, there were some folk in Mudfog
    Who resented the elephants' fame,
Their lives were so grim and their brains were so dim,
    And they needed somebody to blame.

They stood in the Mudfog elections
    And ranted and raved on the telly:
'You've got to be firm with a stone pachyderm,
    Our watchword is *Not on Your Nelly*!'

'We'll be swamped,' said their Florida spokesman,
    'They're animals under the skin,
Once they've heard we're a soft touch in Mudfog
    We'll have herds of them trying to get in!'

Each night in the town's evening paper
    The letters were worried and vexed:
'It's time our friend Ganesh was taught how to vanish,
    Or else it's our jobs will be next.'

Some said that their skin was too wrinkled,
    Or else that their trunks were too long,
Unnatural, alien, not local to Mudfog –
    In short that they didn't belong.

The council proposed a solution
    Which they hoped would help sort out the mess,
They gave them permission to stay on condition
    That they tried to stand out a bit less.

'Do you have to be such a strange colour?
    Do elephants have to be tall?
Could your trunks be a little bit briefer?
    And why can't your ears be more small?

To be honest, those tusks are just wasted
    On creatures with no sense of price,
Your bums require slimming, your toe-nails need trimming,
    And to eat with your nose isn't nice.

We know you've a right to be different,
    We respect this, as everyone does,
But they say "when in Rome", so now Mudfog's your home,
    Why can't you become more like us?'

The elephants listened in silence
    Then they turned and walked slowly away,
And the only reminder they came here at all
    Is that Mudfog's now elephant grey.

Sunlight and Heat

'Imagination here has very ample scope in fancying a coming day when the bare fields we were then traversing will be covered with a busy multitude and numerous vessels crowding to these banks denote the busy Seaport.'

(Joseph Pease, 1828)

'We have not much of a past to speak of, but we look forward to having a great future.'

(Major Dixon, 1887)

'perhaps in another fifty years or more, this hideous mushroom town will have sunk back again into the arms of Mother Earth.'

(Douglas Goldring, 1925)

'Middlesbrough, a godforsaken "Blade Runner" kind of place.'

(Kate Atkinson, 2002)

I

The Pennine rains begin their homeward course
Like Teesdale salmon swimming to the sea,
From Cross Fell, Cow Green, Cauldron Snout, High Force,

The river is impatient to be free,
A wall of water, fit to burst its sides,
A roaring tide of time and History,

Until the hills give way, the flood subsides
Past Barnard Castle, Darlington and Yarm,
Through Thornaby and Stockton, till it slides

Like strong brown ale towards this place of calm
And watery silence, land of becks and brooks,
A swamp, a treeless waste, a lonely farm,

A turnip field, a church, a world of ducks
Ignored by Celts, by Saxons and by Danes,
A 'waste' according to the Domesday Books.

But through this wild and haunted place of rains,
Peg Powler's rotten teeth, the Sockum Worm,
The cold, unpopulated Cleveland plains,

The snaking river wriggles like a sperm
To fertilise the future with desire
And restless change, to leave behind the germ

Of progress, labour, industry and fire.
For even here, where seals and salmon meet,
Necessity and History will conspire

To build an empire out of light and heat,
And burst the banks by turning muck to brass,
And on the river-floor the stones repeat

Their polished lines that say that all things pass,
And nothing is more permanent than grass.

II

A season without rain: the Tees recedes,
Revealing its accumulated slimes –
A muddy archaeology of needs

And hopes, hard work, hard luck, hard folk, hard times,
In which we dig as if to understand
The stony economic paradigms

In which the ocean grinds the past to sand,
The river keeps its secrets as it flows
And tides will never stop at our command.

Two hundred years ago, the census shows
The population here was twenty-five;
Within a hundred years that figure rose

To *ninety thousand*! See them all arrive
From England, Ireland, Scotland, Cornwall, Wales,
A human flood, exhausted but alive;

From Durham, Staffs and Lancashire, the Dales,
Northumberland (and Germany!) they came
Force-marched by hunger, poverty and tales

Of work that lit the River Tees with flame
From iron-works, furnaces and rolling mills,
Till Stygian night was day in all but name.

Prometheus himself once taught the skills
With which they hammered Teesside iron and steel
From Durham coal and stone from Cleveland Hills,

A phoenix rising from the flame's ordeal
Obliterating rosy-fingered dawn,
Until they built a hard-edged commonweal

Within the Vulcan fires of Bolckow-Vaughan.
And so the town of Middlesbrough was born.

III

The story of this town's a neat device
For moralists who think the past must owe
The present some accounting for the price

Of Change, as if the river Tees could flow
Uphill, upstream, in order to forgive
The foolish hills for what they did not know.

This river-bank is where the present lives,
The future is an ocean which can't wait
To swallow up the past's alternatives:

A little town, the well-planned new estate
Of Joseph Pease, a dock, a railway line,
A pottery, a square – a model state;

Or else a classic study in decline,
A 1930s slum-town, workless, broke,
A failed experiment of flawed design;

A gold-rush Klondyke, breathing fire and smoke,
Ironopolis! An infant Hercules!
A commonwealth of work, a field of folk;

Or this one – post-industrial, on its knees,
Awash with crack and smack, that likes to boast
A thriving trade in women by the Tees;

A monastery, perhaps, a staging-post
Where footsore Dunelm travellers can spend
The night, midway to Whitby down the coast;

Or here, beyond the river's hairpin bend,
A wilderness of weeds and broken glass
That marks the town's beginning and its end,

A monument of burned-out cars and grass
In praise of mighty Ozymandias.

IV

Ambition, hunger, struggle, pride and toil –
The story of this town grows by degree,
First iron and steel, then chemicals and oil.

Now they have gone who knows what we shall be?
And which comes first, the raindrop or the stream?
How long's the coal-seam hidden in the tree?

To every age the future choices seem
More urgent and compelling than the last;
We stumble through the present in a dream,

Somewhere between the future and the past,
Between the moorland rainfall and the sea,
We make the world until we have surpassed

Our former selves. In 1853
They looked the Gorgon future in the eyes
And said that by this river We Shall Be,

One Body Politic beneath the skies,
More powerful together than alone.
Such boldness and invention justifies

All those who are forgotten and unknown,
A footnote to the river's turning page,
Who made this windy river bank their own,

Who only thought to earn a common wage,
But built a town of dirt and smoke and fire
That was the very wonder of the age,

A town that spanned both past and future, via
Adventure, vision, enterprise and sweat,
A hell on earth, or else a world entire,

A story that nobody should forget,
An epic tale that isn't over yet.

V

But History is the sum of many choices,
A melody that has no single source,
The river swells with tributary voices,

A cataract that has to run its course.
From tarns collecting melting Pennine snows
On Cross Fell, down through Cauldron Snout, High Force,

The river's story's told in fluid prose:
A half-remembered tale we've heard before,
Unchanged but always changing as it flows

To meet the waves that thrash upon the shore.
As if the cold North Sea can still recall
These hills once slept beneath the ocean floor

Two hundred million years ago; a small
Time for an ocean that has sometimes felt
Volcanic islands rise, and mountains fall.

The Romans passed through here, the Dane, the Celt,
The monks, the Ironmasters – one by one
They passed away. All human empires melt

One day, just like the snow that falls upon
The distant Pennine hills. All that remains
Is this old rusty river, rolling on,

Replenished every morning by the rains;
The wind that blows the past on down the street;
Imagined futures guttering in drains;

The universal need for light and heat;
And far below the river's dirty glass
The stones that on the river-floor repeat

Their polished lines that say that all things pass,
And nothing is more permanent than grass.

Phrase Book

Excuse me, could you tell me the way to the Museum?
Do you belong to a trade union?
I'm sorry, I cannot help you, I am a tourist.
What is the forecast for today?
I am from the DDR.
What happened to my country?
I cannot find it on the map.
I stayed in the Soviet Union last year.
How long do you intend to stay?
What is the purpose of your visit to this country?
Where can I find it?
Is it true your poets write only for each other?
Why do you dislike foreigners?
Do you still have political parties?
Which party is in power?
We have many workers in our factory who belong to the
    Communist Party.
Did you hear of our last strike?
Why are there so many poor people in this country?
You can never be sure of the weather.
It is cold on the streets.
Winter has set in.
What happened to my country?
I cannot find it on the map.
Please help me.
I am lost.
I am English.

Letter to Randall Swingler Part II

I don't know if you got my previous letter
  (For all I know the dead don't read their mail),
But since you've not replied, I thought I'd better
  Make one last try to penetrate the veil;
If you can't write, just use the old planchette
  To let me know what's new inside the whale;
I know you're dead, but corpsing every line
Just makes me feel like Doktor Frankenstein.

It isn't easy writing to a ghost,
  It's hard work sending letters to a void,
Ottava rima turns my brains to toast,
  Unanswered letters leave me quite annoyed,
But though I'd like a message in the post
  Your silence doesn't make me paranoid –
I'm used to corresponding with the dead
Since most of what I write remains unread!

The fact that you are dead is no excuse
  For sounding like the Silence of the Sea,
I know that you tried playing the recluse
  In your last years (perhaps you'd disagree),
But now you're dead I wish you'd reproduce
  Your famous bar-stool repartee for me;
Instead of which you lie there, unimpressed,
While I harangue you like a wedding guest.

All poets, as you know, are sometimes tempted
  To tell themselves the audience doesn't matter,
The page records the world you have attempted,
  And that's not measured by the critics' clatter
(A lie from which I know I'm not exempted),
  But this poem's like a cod without the batter,
A twelve year old without a mobile phone,
An envelope returned, 'address unknown'.

The chances are you'll say you don't remember
  Just what this correspondence is about,
Or why I'm freezing here in late December
  With spade and lap-top, trying to dig you out,
Don't worry, though, I've no plans to dismember
  What's left of you (though if it hurts just shout);
I only want to rearrange your ashes
And talk to you before this lap-top cra

The things I've done for you! Your new *Selected*
  Is out in handsome paperback from Trent;
Please don't be cross that nobody corrected
  The typos in the copy that I sent,
It isn't likely they will be detected,
  The book was such a stunning non-event;
Far worse a fate than any critics' boos
Is when a book comes out to no reviews.

I've tried my best to bring you back to life,
  Because the world could learn from your example,
That's why you're on the slab beneath my knife
  (I only want to take a little sample),
I don't know why you're giving me such strife,
  A word or two from you would be quite ample;
But if you don't reply I promise this'll
Be my last stab at writing verse-epistle.

I dreamed once I was reading from your stuff
  (I know this makes me sound a sad old bore);
The audience loved it, couldn't get enough,
  But there was someone listening by the door
(To be quite honest, he was looking rough),
  He stood there like some ghost from Elsinore,
Then disappeared. Don't ask me how I knew,
But when I woke I knew that it was you.

Unless my rusty Latin's playing tricks
    I think my note was properly addressed –
Poste restante Hades, near the River Styx?
    Or are you on the Islands of the Blessed?
Or with those heroes (Canto XXVI)
    Like Ulysses, whom Dante made Hell's guest,
Condemned to burn in flames for ever more
Because he had the Luck to steal a war?

Your life was like a story out of Homer
    (I know I've tried to make this point before),
At Anzio you breathed in the aroma
    Of burning ships upon the Trojan shore,
Although the term heroic's a misnomer,
    You stared into the Cyclops face of war,
A nobody who walked among the dead
But lived and blinded famous Death instead.

And then the wandering years of guilt and shame –
    The Scylla and Charybdis of despair,
You heard the tempting Siren-song of fame,
    And drank with Lotus-eaters in the bar,
A beggar in disguise who hid the name
    Of anger underneath the rags of war;
If this was peace, you saw no reason why
You shouldn't drink the wine-dark ocean dry.

These days the wars we fight are much more clean,
    Our smart-bombs (like our war-aims) soar much higher,
And though we find it hard to tell between
    A missile silo and a tumble-dryer,
All those destroyed by enemies unseen
    Are glad to know they've died by Friendly Fire;
If war acquired a bad name in the Forties,
You should see what we're doing in the Naughties.

Instead of MAD (which made a sort of sense)
  We've now the doctrine of Pre-emptive Strike,
Which means that in the name of self-defence
  We bomb to bits small countries we don't like,
Whose governments have given us offence
  (The model seems to be the old Third Reich);
And best of all we never come off worst
Because we always hit the bullies first.

That said, there's not much changed since I last wrote,
  The same old stuff – oppression, hunger, war –
In Washington some monkey stole the vote
  That should have gone to President Al Gore,
A democratic trick they now promote
  With their contempt for international law;
If this old dirty world is getting grubbier
It's thanks to corporate crooks like Jeb and Dubya.

In war the USA's the market-leader,
  And now they've launched the world on some crusade
Against a gruesome crew called Al-Qaida,
  Which means the USA can now invade
Just where and when it wants to, gentle reader,
  Such double-talk should make us all afraid.
The power they have is positively feudal
(And Britain is, of course, the White House poodle).

The calendar, meanwhile, is in reverse,
  A Summer's day can bring you out in tumours,
The car you drive is now a kind of hearse,
  The melting Poles are more than swelling rumours,
And though this global warming's getting worse
  We mustn't blame gas-guzzling consumers
For oily White House boffins now espouse
The theory that it's due to farting cows!

I'm writing this in Y2K02,
    Which sounds like somewhere filmed by Ridley Scott;
This century's like a spaceship where the crew
    Have all been eaten up by God knows what,
Adrift in space, we don't know what to do,
    And yet, although we've clearly lost the plot,
The stuff we've packed to take to carry with us
Would even give an Alien the shivers.

Among the monsters breeding in the hold
    Are fierce, revolting, superstitious dreads –
The curse that turns what we most love to gold,
    The xenophobic dogs with many heads,
The stone-faced gods of poverty and cold,
    The pits of polished bones and arrowheads,
The atavistic, empire fires of war,
The horror of the hungry at the door.

Now you are dead, you would be more at ease
    Among the bone-yard culture of our era,
The ghostly lines of hooded refugees,
    The lands laid waste by dragon-tailed chimaera;
'Why this is Hell,' said Mephistopheles,
    The truth of which is daily getting clearer;
Each morning brings more news of life's defeats
Sewn-up in smutty-fingered winding-sheets.

And yet among the brain-dead tabloid stories
    There is one piece of news might make you smile,
You would enjoy the sight of leading Tories
    Committing public suicide in style.
That's not to say that things are hunky-dory,
    Somehow, alas, the new lot's just as vile,
The ruling class, of course, is still in power:
New Labour's Mrs Thatcher's finest hour.

If you've not heard of her, you're bound to later,
  When she and all her cronies turn to dust,
For now I'd rather spare you all the data,
  The chronicle of horror and disgust,
Suffice to say, there's no incinerator
  That's hot enough to roast her to a crust;
They'll need to find some tortures more discerning,
Because, you see, this lady's not for turning.

The left's now down to small, confessing sects
  Who still believe we're in the Final Days;
Their chiliastic confidence reflects
  Impatience with derailments and delays,
A sympathetic reflex which protects
  Their fading hopes from History's iron gaze;
So fans of Trotsky, Stalin, Mao and Blanqui
Ride backwards into History on a donkey.

There's lots more stuff I really should explain,
  Although you probably will not thank me for it.
This poor old world's still going down the drain,
  And typically we've chosen to ignore it;
It's party time, you see (you can't abstain
  Unless you are a joyless, po-faced curate),
And what we call Reality's another
New series of *Celebrity Big Brother*.

Meanwhile a bunch of crazies called the Raelians
  Have said they want to breed a human clone,
They seem to think that we are sprung from aliens
  (I think they got this from *The Twilight Zone*),
And see themselves as latter-day Pygmalians
  Who want to carve the future on the bone
And reproduce themselves till they surpass
The beauty of Narcissus in the glass.

Biography's like cloning, you might say,
    No doubt I've given you some bits of me,
Perhaps I've made too much of your dismay,
    Perhaps I've overdone the late ennui,
Or else perhaps it works the other way
    (Where else should I learn words like *peccavi*?)
It's difficult sometimes to see the line
That separates your failures from mine.

Forgive me then, if I have got you wrong,
    I've tried my bloody best to tell your story
(That's partly why it took so bloody long)
    But if you think I've been too harsh a jury
Or if I've slipped my words beneath your tongue
    I'd rather you don't haunt me in a fury,
It's not my job to air-brush out your flaws
And anyway, your life's no longer yours!

I hope your death is going pretty well,
    That you are thriving on the other side;
Are you knee-deep in fields of asphodel?
    And have you written much since you last died?
Although I don't believe in Heaven or Hell,
    I wonder if you'd care to be my guide?
This means you playing Virgil to my Dante,
Since what I know of Death is pretty scanty.

Does Death contain a long-dead-poets' corner?
    Do writers have to hang out when they're dead?
Is Hell like being locked inside a sauna
    With all the writers whom you've never read?
Eternity must be a bloody yawner
    And Death acquire a special kind of dread
If you're obliged to share eternal splendour
Cooped up with Eric Blair and Stephen Spender!

If you've been writing poetry of late,
    I wonder if you'd care to let me see it?
A dead good book of dead-poems might create
    A publishing phenomenon (albeit
The chances are you're somewhat out of date).
    On second thoughts, I cannot guarantee it –
You see the poetry scene's already heaving
With writers who it seems are scarcely breathing.

I'm generalising now, and know I oughtn't,
    But honestly, how else should I convey it?
If you've got nought to say, it's not important,
    As long as you can stand up or deejay it,
The lifelessness of poetry's a portent,
    It isn't what you say, it's how you say it;
So bold new books from Picador and Faber
Hold up a gorgeous mirror to New Labour.

I hope that you have found a smoky bar
    That only serves dead Reds (and good red wine),
A room above The Laughing Commissar
    Where drinks are on the house for auld lang syne,
Where you can *épater les morts bourgeois*,
    Where every night the barmaids look divine,
And dead drunk comrades drink to better days
Where old Fitzrovia meets with Père Lachaise.

Perhaps you'd like to raise a glass or two
    And give your fans a modest little wave,
Accept a drink to toast the Life of you,
    Because, although alas, I've had to waive
The royalties, your Life is nearly due;
    Conclusive proof there's life beyond the grave,
And that, as Joe McCarthy should have said,
It's better to be read than to be dead.

Five years you took to write and then five more
　　To find someone who'd put you in a book,
At times I thought you'd end up in the drawer,
　　That you and I had really come unstuck;
I'm glad to say my fears were premature,
　　Cos – thanks to MUP – we're both in luck:
Though fifty quid a throw is still a bummer,
You're coming out in hardback in the Summer!

I hope that this time round you'll get the breaks,
　　That you'll enjoy the stupid world's applause;
In one sense all biographies are fakes,
　　They follow their own simplifying laws,
So if your Life contains a few mistakes
　　At least this time you know they're mine, not yours!
But if you like it better than the real one
At fifty quid a time you'll have to steal one.

I've said enough, and really must conclude
　　Before this verse-form puts me in a trance,
I'd like to think that you'll be well reviewed,
　　And yet I don't suppose you stand a chance,
In fact I'd like to bet we'll get well screwed,
　　Or frozen by the critics' Gorgon glance;
I should have put you in a period folly
The sort that makes all Commies look a wally.

You see the world's still full of sneaks and narks,
　　Enthusiastic converts like St Paul,
Who earn their keep by ridiculing Marx
　　And all the hopes which once held them in thrall
And dedicate themselves to serving sharks
　　Who don't believe in anything at all:
The kind of stuff – if you'll forgive my candour –
That's simply Cold War bollocks-propaganda.

You'd think the Cold War's victors would be calmer,
　　Considering how handsomely they won it,
Instead they need to keep alive the drama
　　Like some long-running drawing-room whodunit,
It looks to me like pretty dodgy karma
　　When this world's not enough for those who run it,
Suggesting they're still haunted by the spectre
That one day they will get it up their recta.

Goodbye, old friend, it's time I went to bed,
　　Because, although you may say I'm a dreamer,
I'd like to sleep as soundly as the dead
　　And put to sleep this damned *ottava rima*;
To be quite frank, it's doing in my head,
　　This ABABABCC schema,
But after writing this eight-line repeater
I know my dreams will come in rhyme and metre.

P.S. Your final proofs have just arrived,
　　They're staring at me, waiting to be checked,
A proof of sorts that says we both survived
　　The perils of the Life through which we've trekked;
And now it's done I'm feeling, well, deprived,
　　If you don't feel the same I can't object:
But if you hate your Life you'll have to lump it;
We'll talk about it at the final trumpet.

Comrade Laughter's Joke Book

We had a laugh in Ravensbruck,
We split our sides in Bursa,
On Roben Island life was droll,
In Pankrac jokes got worser,
And though in Turi we were witty
Those Gulag gags were really pretty
   shitty.

Comrade Laughter: Last Known Whereabouts

Although this grinning photo proves
That you were in Grenada,
Where all they had was ridicule
To fight the Yank invader,
The day that poor Maurice was tried
The Revo's sunlit laughter died
   inside.

Alchemical

'Shadow girders faced with sun
Shimmer like heaped bullion.'
(Tony Harrison, 'Newcastle is Peru')

'Materium superabat opus.'
(Ovid, *Metamorphoses*)

Three days beside the River Tyne
  Inside a building whose design
Is T. Dan Smith/Ceauşescu chic;
  Three days in this historic week
When London tells us when and how
  (If we are good) they will allow
The North its own Creation myth
  (Though not the one by T. Dan Smith).

A time of change, as power devolves
  And time's glass exit door revolves,
And Arsène Wenger wins the double,
  And Peter Reid's in serious trouble,
The Toon are in the Champions' League,
  New Labour's suffering from fatigue,
And 'futurorg' means Northern Arts.
  One story ends, another starts.

Three days up North to make new friends
  Or enemies (it all depends),
Where rivalries are dusted down
  And washed away with pints of brown.
Three days away from work and home
  To maybe let your fancy roam.
So put your wallet in the kitty –
  This Tyneside is a party city!

In pubs and clubs, the steps of banks,
   In bus-stops, chip-shops, taxi-ranks,
The town is changed on weekend nights
   By followers of Bacchus' rites,
Till each Toon Army nymph and satyr
   Turns ten-pint chaos into matter
Before (or after) they beget
   What starts in beer and ends in sweat.

This is the striped-pyjama Toon
   Where black and white go well with Broon,
And kids and dogs are christened Shearer;
   With one foot in the modern era,
And one still in the history books,
   This place is in a state of flux;
One night the Queen, the next Bob Dylan –
   Is change the hero or the villain?

The Tyne is now a building site
   Where muddy chaos turns to light
Reflected on the golden cranes
   That hang the clouds out when it rains.
Because, this year Y2K2,
   Newcastle grows more like Peru,
And thanks to Deutschmarks, Francs and Krone,
   Now Gateshead thinks it's Barcelona!

Between the Tyne's unblinking Eye,
   The A1 Angel in the sky,
They're spending fifty million quid
   To boost the Cultural City bid,
Erecting temples by the Tyne
   To prove we are not philistine
And show the world we cannot wait
   Until the year 2008.

If Newcastle is El Dorado,
　　The Baltic wants to be the Prado;
This really *controversial* venue
　　Will serve a controversial menu
In studio and catering space
　　(And no doubt those who run the place
With five new controversial galleries
　　Will get paid controversial salaries).

But those in search of Montezuma,
　　May need to keep a sense of humour;
No matter how the funders will it,
　　The question is – how will they fill it?
Once lost inside the Baltic Mills
　　(Like Fitzcaraldo in the hills!)
The golden footsteps of Solano
　　May lead you face down in the guano.

At least the dream of gold's a sign
　　The stones are turning in the Tyne,
For even here change will not wait,
　　As Europe's last One Party State
Begins to threadbare at the seams
　　And nothing's quite the way it seems,
And would-be mayors end their campaigns
　　With nought to lose – except their chains.

Here bars serve up Post-Modern retro,
　　And sheep can travel on the Metro,
And far beneath the North Sea floor
　　Dark matter grows behind a door,
And Darwin's monkeys stand for mayor,
　　And thanks to pious Tony Blair
Now Genesis is taught in college
　　As though it's scientific knowledge.

Creation myths like this are tired
  And leave a lot to be desired,
Especially when their tellers hark
  Back to the superstitious dark
We once escaped (and even worse
  When paid for by the public purse).
And yet, Creation myths contain
  A truth which science can't quite explain.

The narratives which flatter gods
  From Genesis to Hesiod's
Begin with spells like *'fiat lux'*
  Transforming matter from the flux;
The stuff of every Mythopoeia
  Makes something out of nought appear,
Transforming silence, formless night,
  To beauty, music, substance, light.

So early humans stood apart
  From Nature by the use of art,
Creating tools from sculpted bone,
  Imposing order stone by stone,
Creating their Creation myths
  Of chaos tamed by neoliths,
Asserting from the very start
  All worlds begin and end with art.

So painting, dancing, story, song,
  Collectivised and made us strong;
The pulse that organised our labours
  Turned hungry loners into neighbours;
The harvest in, the auroch caught,
  By rhythm of both hands and thought,
Till round the fire the clan is warmed,
  By magic, art and work transformed.

All art's a way to conjure change
   And make familiar what was strange;
Bewitching chaos into shape's
   What separates us from the apes.
So Orpheus's song uprooted trees
   And Daedalus rose on the breeze
And Galatea leapt from the stone
   To kiss her maker, flesh and bone.

And yet all artists learn one day
   It sometimes works the other way,
There are some spells you can't reverse
   That sometimes leave you feeling worse:
Like Psyche when she fell for Cupid,
   Left in the dark and feeling stupid.
Or Midas turning all to brass,
   Or Lucius (*The Golden Ass*),

Who, when the magic went all wonky
   Was turned into a dancing donkey.
Though he's a hero in disguise
   It's maybe one you recognise.
Perhaps you know the cut-throat clan
   Who hitched him to their caravan?
The carrot and the sharpened stick
   That made him turn just one more trick?

The moral of this donkey fable
   Is read the small-print on the label;
Or else you'll end up jumping hoops
   To satisfy a eunuch troupe,
Submitting hopeless prayers to Isis
   To get you through a funding crisis,
The cheers and jeers that sound the same,
   The ass who always gets the blame.

Like Lucius, all artists try
　To learn the magic formulae,
The language of divine afflatus:
　Empowerment and Beacon Status
The Arts in Health/Education,
　And Partnerships, Regeneration,
Diversity and Artist-led,
　Entitlement and EAZ,

And SRBs and RDAs,
　LSPAs and CPAs
And ESF and CPD,
　BVPP and EDP,
The dreaded letters P and I –
　The acronyms just multiply
(And now there's even one of them
　Spelled A.C.R.O.N.I.M.!).

Pump Priming Grants and Regional Boards,
　Soft Infrastructures, Grants, Awards,
Best Value audit, Charter Marks,
　Percent for Art and Leisure Parks,
And Heritage and tourist trails,
　And projects putting poets in gaols,
And YOTA, RALP and outreach schemes,
　And Public Art and private dreams.

And when you are not writing bids,
　And entertaining screaming kids,
Arranging transport, making kites,
　And panicking on opening nights,
Composing blurbs and press-releases,
　And picking up the broken pieces
Each time the politicians sneeze,
　Negotiating artists' fees,

Attending meetings, counting heads,
   And selling tickets, hotel beds,
And going to Best Practice Days,
   And lost inside the funding maze,
And putting chairs out, booking bands,
   (Or poets no one understands),
Creating masks and meeting trains,
   You just hope nobody complains . . .

And just in case that's not enough,
   It's now assumed that art's the stuff
To solve the problems of our time –
   Like unemployment, health and crime,
Inclusion, disaffected lads,
   The self-esteem of single dads,
Sex Education, drugs campaigns –
   And still, we hope, art entertains!

Don't be surprised then, if you're tired,
   Or find next week that you've been fired,
This is a game that can't be won.
   The job you do – it can't be done!
And yet, although pure gold exists
   Without the help of alchemists,
Perhaps there's other kinds of treasure
   Too valuable to weigh or measure.

So next week when you're back at t' mill
   Recall this conference, if you will;
Three days up North for serious thinking,
   Debate, good food and serious drinking,
To talk and listen and exchange
   Grim stories of the pace of change
Within arts-funding while you scowl
   At Tessas Blackstone and/or Jowell.

Perhaps you'll go home feeling fresher
    And more prepared to face the pressure,
Or chilled-out by the purring tones
    Of conference-gossip, mobile phones,
And lots of PR spin and flannel
    From well-dressed speakers on the panel
And earnest speeches from the floor
    You've heard so many times before.

Perhaps you'll stay a day or two
    And see what weekend Geordies do,
And leave high-minded culture-chat,
    Arts Council this, Arts Council that,
And taste the culture of the street
    Where different kinds of magic meet,
Where all things can be bought and sold
    To turn base metal into gold.

If you want music, matter, light
    Try Jesmond Road on Friday night,
Where every kind of demographic
    Goes singing through the dancing traffic.
Perhaps the long-sought panacea
    Of alchemy tastes just like beer,
Perhaps all art is just a form
    Of sorcery to keep us warm,

Perhaps Newcastle *is* Peru,
    Perhaps Creation myths *are* true,
Perhaps collective magic's force
    Is irrespective of its source.
It isn't who supports this art
    (That puts the horse behind the cart)
But what all art – and you – support:
    A whole world conjured out of nought.

We'll Go No More A-raving

'Man, being reasonable, must get drunk;
The best of life is but intoxication.'
                    (Byron, *Don Juan*)

In his leather boots and cloak
    He was looking ellish cool,
Such a drop-dead gorgeous bloke
    Dropped in drop-dead Hartlepool,

Like the early Elvis Presley
    Crossed with Eighties New Romantic
(In the queue outside the Wesley
    All the girls were going frantic!).

He was coming out of Churchill's
    When he says, like, on a whim
That if we will be his Virgils
    Then the drinks are all on him.

Well, we didn't hesitate,
    Caught the next bus we could find
Heading for the Headland Gate –
    O let joy be unconfined!

So we started in the Station
    With a round of Newky Brown
Then we hit the Corporation
    Where we sank another down;

In the Union we drank sherry,
    In the Fisherman's spumante,
In the Durham we got merry
    On some bottles of chianti;

We drank cider in the Sun,
  We swigged bourbon in the rain,
In the Grapes we had some fun
  Mixing Camerons and champagne;

In the Lion we drank Martini,
  In the Alma, rum and black,
Youth and Pleasure's like a Genie –
  Once they're out they won't go back.

In the Masons we drank Bud
  (So we must have been well-pissed!),
Drinking toasts to old King Ludd,
  And the raising of the wrist;

After dancing in the Raby
  To a bar-room hokey cokey,
And a round of 'Bye Bye Baby'
  On the Greyhound's karaoke,

In the Bridge he somehow jammed
  The old juke-box up with cash,
Playing endless Doors, the Damned,
  Spandau Ballet and the Clash.

We plays snooker in the Clyde,
  In the Borough we watch telly
(But he'll not see the inside
  Of the King's Head nor the Welly).

In the tap-room of the Anchor,
  Well, he nearly starts a fight
Shouting, 'Southey is a wanker'
  And 'Lord Castlereagh's a shite!'

Now his nibs begins to ramble
  And his speech is getting slurred,
By the time we reach the Campbell
  We can't hear a bleeding word.

In the Cosmo he demanded
  A fresh bowl of Samian wine
(Though by then, well, to be candid,
  He'd have drunk fresh turpentine).

In the Empress we sups mild
  In the Beehive we quaff porter;
In the Lawrenson he smiled
  When he saw the landlord's daughter;

In the Cleveland we drink whisky,
  In the Albert we drink brandy,
In the Klondyke he gets frisky,
  By the Brunswick he's dead randy;

In the Angel, drinking scotch,
  He stands drinks for everyone,
But his mind is on his crotch
  (Like a right old Don Juan);

Between shots of gin and tonic
  And a raucous game of darts,
He starts acting all Byronic
  With a pair of Seaton tarts.

In the Alex he buys drinks
  For a crowd of Headland lasses.
In the Hartlepool he winks
  At the lass collecting glasses,

Then he takes some cans of Stella
  And a carry-out of gin,
With a lass called Annabella
  Round the back of the New Inn.

With his smooth 'On with the dances!'
  And his *obtabilem* passion
He'll screw anyone he fancies
  Like it's going out of fashion.

Next we saw him in his breeches
  On the wall outside the Ship
Making loud poetic speeches
  Re a midnight skinny dip;

Says he's had another whim
  After swigging some retsina,
And he's setting off to swim
  Right across to the marina.

We were standing in the doorway
  Of the Pot House drinking lager
When he tries to swim to Norway
  Like a hero from some saga,

So he dives in with a yelp
  And a lot of coughs and sneezing –
Being a hero's not much help
  When the climate's bloody freezing;

Even gods should stay off nectar
  In the middle of October,
Because no one fears the spectre
  Of Romantics who ain't sober;

If you need a bit of rough
  To turn living into art,
This old frozen world's enough
  To melt any drunken heart.

Steel Giant Threatens to Quit Mudfog

There once was a very big giant,
  A fairy-tale giant made of steel,
He was built by a hard-working people
  To safeguard their town's commonweal.

They'd heard tales of the capital city
  Where the money-faced monsters lurk
That feed upon small towns like Mudfog,
  Devouring their wages and work.

So they laboured to build their colossus,
  And they struggled a century and more,
By day and by night the skies were alight
  With the bright burning hopes of the poor.

They fed it with coal and with iron,
  And they sweetened its brow with their sweat,
They worked and they toiled and they polished and oiled
  Till they thought the steel giant in their debt.

And its legs were as long as a late shift,
  It was hard as a job in the mills,
Its heart was as hot as a furnace,
  Its memory was old as the hills.

But the day came, alas, when the giant
  Decided the town was too small,
For a giant needs gold and adventure
  And doesn't need people at all.

When they heard the steel giant was to leave them
  The people of Mudfog went off it,
'But we made you!' they said, 'you can't leave us for dead,
  Just because you're not making a profit.'

But the steel giant could not be persuaded,
   'I no longer need you,' he scoffed,
'I'm leaving you here, and I'm off to Korea!'
   Then he upped and he went and he offed.

All children know giants are monsters
   Who travel in seven-league boots,
So don't be reliant on a corporate giant
   And small men in oversize suits.

All fairy-tales must have a moral,
   And this one is not rocket-science –
Control of the means of production's
   The best way to stand up to giants.

Why Aye, Minister

Another day, another launch,
　　To supplement the Christmas paunch
With tasty sound-bites, bites to eat,
　　To check the New Year balance-sheet
Of politics in Jan 04,
　　Who's in, who's out, who's for the door,
Who's smiled upon by two-faced Janus,
　　And who's to get it up the anus.

Although this year's a clean, blank page,
　　An infant month of little age,
Already the engagement diary
　　Is filling up – the Hutton Inquiry,
More PFIs, tuition fees,
　　Those missing WMDs.
The poor year's not been born a week,
　　But January's looking bleak.

For you, perhaps, it's one more plate
　　Of dips with which to put on weight,
Another glass or two of claret
　　While listening to someone parrot
On and on about some cause
　　That keeps wild-eyed provincial bores
Awake at night (you know the kind,
　　Whose joy's a blunt-edged axe to grind).

The deal's that while you fill your glasses
　　We butter up the chattering classes;
Enjoy yourself then, try the wine
　　(Matured in vineyards by the Tyne),
Bear with us though, while we advance
　　The reasons why we think the chance
Of Devolution's worth a throw
　　And why the North won't answer *No*.

Of course, a slow news day's our hope,
    A day to lather out with Soap
And TV gossip, show-biz news
    Designed to lift the New Year blues,
Low-level features, just enough
    To fill the page, but not the stuff
To fill tomorrow's phone-in shows
    Or stimulate immortal prose.

The media-jungle being Darwinian
    We hope that you, who shape opinion,
Might write about our cause, perhaps
    (You'll find the North East on your maps) –
You know the place, where folk talk funny,
    And no one seems to have much money,
A stunted race of North East Gollums.
    With which to decorate your columns.

I'm sorry if that sounded chary,
    It's just that London's pretty scary;
For small-town folk from the North East
    This is the Belly of the Beast;
Like Duncan dropping in on Cawdor,
    Or Frodo creeping into Mordor,
Like Daniel in the lion's den,
    We doubt we'll see our homes again.

You see, us simple Northern folk,
    We rarely get down to the Smoke,
Like rabbits who don't leave the hutch,
    Or Hobbits who don't travel much;
And yet we've marched, like refugees,
    Across the Tyne, the Wear, the Tees,
Asylum-seekers, you might say,
    Inside the old mad-house UK.

The difference is, we're 'genuine' –
  We want to exit, not get *in*!
Well not quite *exit*, that's too strong,
  The UK's where we all belong,
It's just that London has some powers
  That we believe should be, well, ours,
We want to take them, that's the plan
  (Though only if you say we can!).

The problem is, we're thick and broke,
  A stand-up comic's easy joke;
The land of *Viz* and ghostly ships,
  George Reynolds, Sedgefield fish and chips,
Of Ant and Dec and Chubby Brown –
  Each second-hand and hand-me-down
Cartoon-strip North hints with a smirk
  That Devolution just won't work.

Sometimes it seems that you contrive
  To think that the M25
Is like a kind of Chinese Wall
  Beyond which there's no life at all,
A desert labelled Here Be Dragons
  Beyond the line of covered-wagons,
A wall designed by Maginot
  Beyond which media folk daren't go.

But we've some cartoons of our own,
  A set of clichés set in stone:
Tax-dodging toffs from public school
  Who think the North means Liverpool,
Soft Southern bastards, on the make,
  A town of rent-boys on the take;
If you think Northern folk are Orcs
  At least we eat with knives and forks!

We're here to ask you to consider
  How truth goes to the lowest bidder,
It's hard for North to speak with South
  When both our feet are in our mouth.
But North and South are changing fast,
  We're less divided by the past,
From now on we're like friendly neighbours
  (Where Old Corruption meets New Labour's).

While Europe's last One Party State
  Begins to discombobulate,
Our culture grows more uniformly
  (Like ACNE, or something by Gormley);
We act geet cool in Baltic galleries
  Where mushy-peas are low on calories,
And greet the new Anish Kapoor
  With cries of 'Shut the art-house door!'

As power devolves both up and down
  It's more a verb and less a noun,
It benefits all those who lose it
  No less than those who start to use it
(Like Christmas presents gild the giver);
  Give us the chance and we'll deliver
A levelled and devolving state
  Served up like dips upon a plate.

Bring government a little nearer
  To those who call their pit-bulls Shearer,
And let decision-making rest
  With those who know the region best –
It's not exactly rocket-science
  Or Zapatista-like defiance,
OK, it's not the Magna Carta,
  So what? But it will do for starters.

For once invited to express
  A choice between a *No* and *Yes*,
We're halfway to that noble dawn –
  The Ashes won by Michael Vaughan,
Success in Portugal 04,
  More sex, less rain, and no more war,
More holidays, more pay, less stress,
  Our watchword always, Yes! Yes! Yes!

We're positive, we're for, we're *pro*,
  Unlike all those who just say *No*,
Like King Canute upon the shore
  Resisting change for ever more,
Like Brezhnev in the politburo,
  Or Mrs Thatcher on the Euro,
Ian Paisley, Ariel Sharon,
  And Charles de Gaulle *qui disait 'Non!'*

As if the tides of change will cease
  And sand give up its slow increase
Because *No* bodies will it so
  Like Carlyle's 'Everlasting No',
St Augustine's *sed noli modo*,
  Or Bilbo trying to trick old Frodo;
As if the fear of sharing power
  Could stop the clock for just one hour.

That's not to say that saying *Yes*
  Itself will guarantee success.
Devolving power, by definition's
  Not easy for some politicians,
And politicians need to know
  It's going to mean some letting go;
If not, a regional assembly
  Will take as long to build as – Wembley.

This club is thus a fitting choice
  In which to give our *Yes* its voice.
A common wealth – the words combine
  The hopes of 1649,
Of Commonweal and Common Rights,
  Of wartime by-election fights,
Of winds of change – a common pattern
  In which all hierarchies flatten.

Democracy requires no less
  Than citizens who answer *Yes*,
Or as we say up North, to you
  (Cos we're all Europeans noo):
Senz'altro, claro, mebbes, *oui*,
  Suppose so, *da, sim*, OK, *si*;
Of course, *por supuesto*, we cry,
  Ja natürlich, bien sur – why aye!

Comrade Laughter's Moscow Tour

You would die laughing if you saw
The jokes they run in TASS,
Old Yeltsin wears a clown's red nose
And Putin's just a gas;
They'd be the death of you, you'd bust
A gut with laughter's tears, or just
    disgust.

Comrade Laughter Tries Slapstick

D'you hear the one about the man
Who said that it's a farce
When History repeats itself
And ends up on its arse?
Though sit-coms entertain the masses,
Still History kicks the working classes'
    asses.

Exciting Times in Mudfog

If you believe the ancient Chinese curse
    That interesting times are always grim,
Election nights put curses in reverse –
    The chances of excitement here are slim.

No issues here to set the world alight,
    The parties stretch from average to medium,
As though they really try with all their might,
    To send us all to sleep with hype and tedium.

The more they claim that this election's vital,
    The less that anybody gives a toss
Which intellectual lightweight wins the title,
    And victory's just another name for loss.

The more they try to feed us fibs and lies,
    The more they try their best to reassure us,
The more we sleep because – surprise, surprise –
    Election nights in Mudfog simply bore us.

Who cares about their futile panto capers
    When you could be tucked up asleep in bed?
When you can wait until the morning papers
    To learn that Mudfog politics is dead.

So if you still believe that Chinese curse,
    If interesting times still make you panic,
Remember that things always could get worse,
    You could be fast asleep on the Titanic.

Nee Bovver

Now Tony Blair has drained the world of colour,
   And everyone's New Labour and Post-Mod,
When literary life could hardly get much duller –
   Thank God that there's still room for chaps like Rod.
There's some, no doubt, suspect him mad or jealous,
   And those who think him quaint or simply odd,
Perhaps his violent threats are over zealous,
   You may believe he talks a load of cod –
But Rod enjoys a bit of aggravation,
   He guards the gate without the high-walled quad,
A cross between a poodle and alsatian,
   That's one part nodding dog, part diplopod;
A would-be Mr Muscle and a critic,
   A bouncer with the body of a god,
A doorman with a wit that's troglodytic
   (You only enter if he gives the nod).
Don't mess with Rod, if you can't put your fist up,
   He may be short, but Rod's a well-built bod,
And whether he is sober or just pissed-up
   His pen's as subtle as a cattle prod.
A dickhead with the patience of a hard-on,
   A prick that just can't wait to shoot his wad,
Our Rod's the biggest weed in Covent Garden,
   The plumpest little pea inside the pod.
He may appear a harmless little bleeder,
   A bothersome and bumptious little sod,
But God knows Rod's an energetic weeder,
   Who isn't merely acting on his tod;

His world-historic task is to determine
   Who's in, who's out and who is for the quod,
Dismissing us provincial types as vermin
   Fit only for the poetry-cleansing squad.
Rod knows just how to order into silence
   The rank outsiders throwing stones at God,
Provincials whom he cows with threats of violence,
   Like wood-imps on the run from PC Plod.

What B.L. Coombes once called the Falling Tower
   Was long ago rebuilt by chaps like Rod,
Who climb the well-worn steps of class and power
   By counting all the hands on which they've trod.
His Glasgow kisses underline the moral
   That all who's not from London is a clod,
A rule with which you're not supposed to quarrel
   For if you do you'll feel the wrath of Rod.
The lesson's clear for all provincial hicks,
   Whose place is well defined in Hesiod:
Our lot's to live contented in the sticks –
   If only you will spare us from the Rod.

Oh Well

If you want to be hip and cool
  And choose a life of wild excess,
If you skipped games when still at school
  And left your bedroom in a mess,
The poet's life should be your goal –
Cos poetry's just like rock 'n' roll.

Forget the strutting rock-star stuff,
  The hair-brush mike and air guitar,
If you really want success enough
  If you want to be a superstar,
If you want to play the Hollywood Bowl,
Then poetry is your rock 'n' roll.

The cadillacs and limousines!
  The private jets and screaming fans!
The laser-shows, dry-ice machines,
  The champagne crates and yachts in Cannes,
It might seem like you're on the dole,
But poetry's just like rock 'n' roll.

The groupies, drugs and porno-queens,
  The dressing-rooms that end up smashed,
The re-hab clinics, tabloid scenes,
  The hotel rooms that poets have trashed!
No wonder poets lose control –
They live the life of rock 'n' roll!

We've greatest hits and farewell tours,
  And some who still prefer it folky,
So many rebels without a cause
  And some who mime to karaoke,
But everyone knows from pole to pole
That poetry's just like rock 'n' roll.

We've New Gen idols and Steps-like clones,
   We've chubby Elvis look-alikes,
We've bar-hall queens who sound like Sloans
   And one-hit wonders no one likes,
But nobody cares, if you've got soul,
Cos poetry's just like rock 'n' roll.

We've cool jazz cats and New Age dubbers,
   House DJs and ageing punks,
Fading hippies and strungout clubbers,
   Hip-hop rappers and hopeless drunks –
O the life of a poet takes its toll
Cos poetry's just like rock 'n' roll.

But most just play in tribute bands
   In weekend pubs and smoky bars,
With riffs we learned at second-hand,
   Content to dream of being stars,
To know that poetry's got fuck all
To do with, well, with – rock 'n' roll.

Romeo Beckham

What's in a name? That which we call a rose
    By any other name would smell as sweet –
And yet as every Rose West surely knows
    There are some flowers whose names you can't repeat.
While some of us can grow into a name
    The names you get when you're inside the womb
Can either prove to be your claim to fame
    Or else they can become a kind of doom.
And though a doubly famous name as yours –
    A star-crossed lover *and* a football hero –
No doubt will open lots and lots of doors
    From Manchester to Rio de Janeiro,
I hope that you will sometimes be allowed
To slip outside and join the nameless crowd.

Mudfog Goes Bananas

The ballot boxes are all in,
   The crowds are going ape,
As in a photo-finish count
   The winner breasts the tape,

Then thumps his breast in victory
   To claim this late-night thriller,
For Mudfog's voted for a Mayor
   Resembling a gorilla.

Although it may seem comical
   To London media folk,
To citizens of Mudfog town
   Our leadership's no joke.

He may look like a chimpanzee,
   He may act like a fool,
He may sound like some nightmare
   Dreamed up by Pierre Boulle,

But it's not his fault if he's dumb,
   He can't help being a chimp,
According to the jungle law
   At least he's not a wimp.

In fact he is a primitive
   Just like Jean-Jacques Rousseau's,
A noble savage standing tall,
   With hair between his toes.

He may be stupid, but he's ours,
   And not some Millbank flunkey.
If he's got fleas, he's proud of them:
   A proper Mudfog monkey.

There's something in a simian
  That puts us at our ease,
Reminds us that it's not that long
  Since we were climbing trees,

That after all we're relatives,
  We share the DNA;
From King Kong down to Dubya
  These brutes are here to stay.

Some say that it's embarrassing
  When voters break the mould,
That people shouldn't vote unless
  They vote the way they're told.

While others say our critics
  Have got a bloody nerve,
That voters only ever get
  The leaders they deserve;

Democracy's a funny thing,
  They only want your vote
If you vote for the monkey with
  Their rosette at its throat.

And there are those who argue that
  The voters were perplexed,
Because it's sometimes hard to tell
  One monkey from the next.

While Labour apes the Tories
  The day will come around
When folk will vote for those who drag
  Their knuckles on the ground.

Meanwhile there are psephologists
  And Darwinists who think
The Mayor of Mudfog may turn out
  To be the Missing Link,

The proof that progress can be stopped
  And put into reverse,
And that though things are pretty bad
  They'll keep on getting worse.

Banana-skin republics work
  Like any human zoo,
If you throw people peanuts they'll
  Make monkeys out of you.

One final joke on which to choke,
  A pretzel-shaped reminder:
We may know who the monkeys are,
  But who's the organ grinder?

Crumbs!

Some days are good, some days are bad,
 And some are best forgotten,
There's kids who make you really mad
 Or leave you feeling rotten,
But you can make it after break
So long as someone's brought in cake.

Each Friday at King's Manor School
 You find the local fauna,
Like starving creatures round a pool
 They gather in the corner
And one by one prepare to take
The ritual of the Friday cake.

Between the tales of kids from hell
 And colleagues who are crazy,
The Freudian dreams of Isabel,
 The folk from Royston Vazey,
You know that you are still awake
If someone offers you some cake.

If you're not sure how French kids swear
 Or when to paragraph,
If you can't conjugate *Ta mère*
 Or laugh at senior staff,
If teaching gives you stomach-ache,
Then you should try some Friday cake.

The Black Cats may be going down,
 Last year's results were poor,
The world is bullied by a clown
 Who wants another war –
But half-term's here, for heaven's sake,
And teaching's just a piece of –

Included

1

Another week, another school,
  Another bloody test of wills,
Another bunch of bloody kids
  (A bloody way to pay the bills).
Five days of teaching poetry,
  Five days in which, to be precise,
No matter how you lesson-plan
  You know you're skating on thin ice,
Attempting to enthuse some kids
  Who'll welcome you with frank dismay,
'Reluctant readers' who hate books
  And probably think that poetry's *gay*.
And yet this morning's bright with frost,
  The flooded meadows by the road
Are filigreed with patterned ice
  And icing-sugar where it's snowed:
The image of an unspoiled world,
  An unread book, an early start,
The promise of the week's new page,
  Unprinted yet by work or art.

2

Amazing kids! Fantastic school!
  Where every child's a budding poet,
And every budding child's a reader
  (Although of course they may not know it).
If only every working day
  Could be as satisfying as ours,
If only every school could be
  A hot-house for such vivid flowers.
In just five hours we have produced
  Some rhyming stories by Year 9s,

A blessing-poem for new-born kids,
    Year 7's acrostic Valentines,
Some geometric free-verse shapes
    (First lesson Monday morning Maths!),
A gangsta rap about Macbeth,
    And rhyming songs with lots of laughs.
Word soon gets out – the other kids
    Can smell the poems in the room,
Persuaded by the blossom stink
    To think the Meadows are in bloom.
I don't know why I worried now,
    These Meadows kids are just the best,
Creative, natural artists all;
    It's safe to say I'm dead impressed.

3

If Monday was a buzzing day,
    It's fair to say today was not,
It's been a bloody dreadful day,
    In which I simply lost the plot.
Just when I thought I had it made,
    And that these kids were really nice,
I felt the ground beneath me crack
    And I was falling through the ice.
These meadows are a wilderness,
    The stony ground where nothing grows,
A desert where the spirit dies,
    And verse becomes four-lettered prose.
The very kids who yesterday
    Grew words like wings and flew like gods,
Have somehow been transformed to sour,
    Unwilling, grumpy, little sods.
To say they're wild's to be too kind –
    Untameable, more like, or feral,
If you go to The Meadows School
    To be quite blunt, it's at your peril.

4

And yet, and yet, and yet, and yet,
  I know that's only half the story,
I hope that I will not forget
  The moment when, quite *ex tempore*,
Young Darren spoke with tongues of fire
  A song that pulsed straight from the heart,
As frail and lovely as the bird
  He turned into a work of art.
As if to prove that even here,
  Just when things couldn't get much worse,
That even here, *especially* here,
  Survives the magic art of verse.
How far away the world of books
  And poetry must seem to those
Who never see their lives in print –
  And so the disaffection grows.
'Inclusion' is a mouthful word,
  Its meanings though can be denuded:
When you're convinced the world's not yours
  You know that you have been excluded.

5

'The Meadows School' perhaps suggests
  The kind of place a dreamy child
Might blossom forth – and so they do,
  I've seen them grow both green and wild –
And yet the rarest flowers grow
  Below the meadow's uncut grass,
The tender flowers that grow between
  The weeds of poverty and class.
The lesson that I've learned this week
  Is not the one I thought I'd planned,
An easy one to put in words
  But difficult to understand:

That silence is the common tongue
  Of those whom finer speech traduces,
That anger is an unread book;
  That these are reasons, not excuses;
The fewer words a poet has
  The more each word becomes important;
That poetry's like trespassing,
  You sometimes end up where you oughtn't.

6

It's Friday afternoon at last,
  I'm driving home, too tired to think,
Exhilarated, humbled, knacked
  (And looking forward to a drink).
I wish that I could say the sun's
  Begun to shine on Spennymoor,
But it will take more art than this
  To make these frozen meadows thaw.
For art is indivisible,
  And poetry belongs to all,
A meadow held in common, not
  A garden closed behind a wall.
And poetry's a common art
  That grows best out of common words,
Collective magic on the wing,
  Like setting free imprisoned birds.
Three cheers then for the Meadows kids
  This frozen Friday afternoon,
I'm proud that you included me;
  Goodbye and thanks – I'll see you soon.

On the Re-making of *Goodbye Mr Chips*

And so we reach another end of term,
  Wrung out, hung out and far too tired to mention;
Demoralised, exhausted and infirm,
  It's times like these you hope you'll get that pension
Before the zimmer-frame and plastic hips,
And you begin resembling Mr Chips.

With every year the students come and go,
  And every term you keep on getting older,
Each register's a kind of ghostly show,
  A line of disappointments at your shoulder,
And school's a pit of scorpions and whips –
An early scene from *Goodbye Mr Chips.*

And yet there is a Chips in every teacher,
  Fulfilled, hard-working, patient and concerned,
A fondly thought-of, dedicated creature
  Whom one day kids might thank for what they learned.
The day you feel that Chips-like sense eclipse
You know that it is time to cash your chips.

To educate the young's a noble calling,
  You don't become a teacher for the pay;
Though governments insist the standard's falling
  And there are kids who fill you with dismay,
Some days the mask of cynicism slips
And you're caught smiling – just like Mr Chips.

Though teaching has a strange linguistic history
  (Which is it – *educare* or *ducere*?)
The teacher's job is not a bloody mystery
  (It's just the bloody children who are scary!).
Put simply – to avoid apocalypse
The world must honour folk like Mr Chips.

And so as you begin your Christmas truce
   I hope that you enjoy a proper break;
Instead of wondering what's the bloody use
   Of what you do, just watch the new re-make
Of *Goodbye Mr Chips* and you'll know why
Old Mr Chips could never say goodbye.

Comrade Laughter in Pantoland

The men in wigs, the girl in drag,
The crowd who shouts, 'Behind you!'
'Oh no he's not!' 'Oh yes he is!'
Are there just to remind you
That History's just a pantomime
Where bad guys get away with crime
   big time.

Comrade Laughter at the Circus

Though any fool can fall off steps,
Be hit with custard pies,
The art of looking foolish is
For History's fools to prize:
How hard it is to fall with style,
Enjoy the joke and all the while
   still smile.

The Icing on the Cake

O frozen, still and silent winter scene!
   A snow-caked mountain caught in tinsel light,
A world in candid miniature, as clean
   And perfect as a frosted Christmas night.
This magic gift was wrapped up weeks ago
   One warm, sweet, Autumn-kitchen afternoon,
   And left to set beneath the winter moon
To catch the fall of icing-sugar snow.

O Christmas cake, O Christmas cake! A chaste
   And soft *tabula rasa* where a child
Might look but never touch, a secret place,
   To lose which we are never reconciled.
And here, between the knife-edged drifts of snow,
   There stands a little lamp-lit house, in which
   There burns such laughter, light and warmth, the rich
And easy happiness we long to know.

But now the heavy-handed ritual slice
   Reveals the brown and spongy earth beneath,
The oven warmth contained below the ice,
   The stony peel that sticks between your teeth,
And then the sudden layer of dismay
   Which means great clods of snow must go to waste,
   The sad and adult taste of almond paste,
Which every child must learn to like one day.

Cross-section of the childhood winter frieze,
   It tells us that there's never long to wait
To taste the loss beneath the fallen trees
   Among the crumbled snow-flakes on the plate.
We eat the world and make ourselves and grow
   Until we have become the world we eat,
   And yet the world holds nothing that's as sweet
As disappointments which we don't yet know.

The Age of Reason, 1973

'Comme tous les songe-creux, je confondis
le désenchantement avec la vérité.'
(Jean-Paul Sartre)

A long way from the miners' strikes
   And Vietnam and oil-price hikes,
The coup in Chile, Wounded Knee,
   The Nixon tapes, the EEC,
Your life's marked out *ad nauseam*,
   By homework, essay and exam
And everything you don't yet know
   That makes you feel that you're *de trop*,
And living's an unopened book,
   A record where the needle's stuck,
And girls are just a foreign land
   Whose language you don't understand,
And weekends are a non-event,
   And every Saturday is spent
Exchanging freedom, time and choice
   For something that you can't invoice
Inside a decorating shop
   Where time slows almost to a stop.

But half-past twelve you're unconfined,
   The taste of paint tins left behind,
To spend what you have not yet earned
   On books whose worth you've not yet learned.
This hour of freedom's your reward
   For Saturdays spent being bored –
Inventing shy, romantic myths
   For sixth-form girls who work in Smith's
While rifling through the album sleeves,
   Or browsing through what Smith's believes
Can be called modern verse upstairs
   (Marc Bolan, Rod McEwan, Pam Ayres),

Or reading biogs on the backs
    Of Penguin Classic paperbacks
Designed to make you understand
    That small-town life's at second-hand,
That books belong to those whose lives
    Are not on hold till half-past five,
And somewhere else there's life and art
    That's richer than a colour-chart.

But book-bound freedom cannot last,
    And far too soon it's twenty-past
And time to go back to the boss,
    A prisoner of matt and gloss,
The nauseous stink of turps and paints,
    The working world's absurd constraints,
Inside a stifling afternoon
    That can't – and doesn't – end too soon.
And if you manage to survive
    From half-past one to half-past five,
The cashing-up and checking stock
    Will keep you there past six o'clock
And halfway through the next ice-age
    Until you get your half-spent wage,
Collect your push-bike and unlock it,
    The Roads to Freedom in your pocket.

Outfaced

'At 50, everyone has the face he deserves.'
(George Orwell)

'My shaving razor's cold and it stings.'
(The Monkees)

Near fifty years you've watched this long-lost twin
   Who watches from the bathroom mirror's glass,
A well-known stranger underneath the skin
   Who never lets a bleary morning pass
Without reminding you you're past your best,
   And that you have already reached the stage
When nothing you can do will help arrest
   The thinning hair and thickening lines of age.

Strange ritual game that starts each working day!
   In which you race each other to the sink
And while you scrape away the stubble-grey
   You stare each other out and never blink.
It's hard to say which anxious lines you've earned
   And which were given like a patronymic,
And anyway by now you should have learned
   Your understudy is a natural mimic.

There's clearly something in this mirror face
   That somehow says you really do not mind
If strangers want to put you in your place
   Announcing who your fizzog brings to mind.
When you were younger, people used to stretch
   Across the railway carriage aisle and say,
'You're Michael Palin's double!' (Cheese Shop sketch),
   'You're just like Michael Yorke in *Cabaret*!'

James Taylor (*Two Lane Blacktop*) was OK,
   But you knew it was getting time to worry
When like a dreaded loop from *Groundhog Day*
   Two strangers said you looked just like Bill Murray;
To think of all the men you could have been,
   Instead of this one life in which you're trapped
(And if Bill Murray's your Platonic twin,
   The Man Who Knew Too Little seems more apt).

Although some children from Years 5 and 6
   Once said you made a perfect matching pair
With David Ginola! (without the tricks,
   The skill, the style, the good looks, or the hair),
The parallel's now usually some old codger
   Who always seems to win it by a nose –
Phil Thompson, Gerard Depardieu and *Bodger* –
   A balding race of ageing Cyranos.

And recently you've met the helpful folk
   Who stop you at the bar to offer gladly,
'You are the spitting image of that bloke,
   The ugly one, from *Men Behaving Badly*.'
These days you really do not want to think
   What monsters they will soon mistake you for –
Something from *Men in Black* or *Monsters Inc*?
   Hell Raiser II, the thing from *Alien IV*?

But as you rinse the shaving foam away
   There is no doppelganger more bizarre
Than this old mug who mirrors your dismay
   And lets you know just who and what you are;
Although you can't escape this stranger's stare
   Or hope that you could ever take his place,
He knows exactly just how much despair
   Dismay and disappointment you both face.

Lost

When you are low on petrol, late and lost,
  And every hillside hairpin looks the same,
And every bridge resembles those you've crossed,
  And hamlets are so brief they have no name;

When one more viaduct's just like all the others,
  And you pass pubs you're sure you can recall,
And each daft sheep's the image of its brothers,
  And every mile's one less before you stall;

When every dry-stone corner's like the last,
  And every incline makes you feel you're slowing,
When each farm's like the one you've just been past,
  It's time to say you don't know where you're going,

And that it doesn't matter which you take,
  Each road will bring you back like all the rest,
That every turn you make's one more mistake,
  And every map's a hopeless palimpsest

Through which the fading contours may be seen
  Of landscapes which you thought you could forget,
And all the unmapped spaces in between
  The unmarked lanes of memory and regret.

There are some roads that will not let you go,
  That lead you always backwards to the start,
Like arteries they regulate the flow
  Of love within a lost and mapless heart.

Done

for Jack, at 18

While others draft and sketch before they start,
  You've always seen what's there beneath the page,
Your concentrated, swift and certain art
  Unfolding slowly till you reach the age
When everyone can see the work is done,
  And can't believe it wasn't there before
  And know that what you've made is something more:
The finished image of an eldest son.

Taller

for Joe, at 18

It's strange to credit now, though I suppose
  There must have been a time when you knew less
Than this old man whose threadbare knowledge shows
  Whenever we play music, football, chess;
But stranger still to watch you as you run
  Into a future where I cannot go,
  To see your shadow grow, and yet still know
The man I'm looking up to is my son.

Too Many Stars to Count

The night's a spangled manuscript
   In which can still be read
A cold and heartless narrative
   That lights the way to bed.
Though planets travel round the sun
   Their orbits never cross,
Illuminating vellum dark
   With comet tails of loss
And half-remembered fairy-tales
   Of cold and lonely light
Whose meaning died too long ago
   To reach us here tonight.

There are so many stars to count
   We don't know where to start;
We travel through the unread dark
   So many years apart
And join the dots between the stars
   In patterns of dismay;
Too much to learn, too little time,
   And too much still to say;
So many starry, midnight plans
   That somehow came unstuck,
Too much hard work and patient love
   And not enough good luck.

And yet tonight it's just enough
   To know this planet's ours,
To climb this hill with both of you
   And count my lucky stars.

After Aragon

1 *A Tapestry of Modern Terror*

The hydra swim across the sky
While swordfish, sharks and steel birds scream;
We recognise the siren dream
In which we know we're going to die.
Gigantic insects thread the air
With comet tails of trailing vapour,
A threat inscribed on bright blue paper
To paint the villages with fire.
A Messerschmitt apocalypse!
A broomstick dance, Walpurgis night,
A Witches' Sabbath in full flight
Around the noon-day sun's eclipse.
Between strange fields and birds of prey
The refugees trudge down the roads,
Lugging their fearful, tearful loads.
The steeple bells won't ring today.
The piles of bedding, the panicked flocks.
The broken statues. The carrion cries.
A sewing machine. A dead man lies
Clutching his stomach. A broken clock.
The lost children, their clothes a mess,
Cowering in ditches from sky-borne danger,
Perched on the shoulders of passing strangers.
A hunchback in a wedding dress.
A bird in a cage, a doll, a shawl.
A feverish man in a cart who is crying
For herbal tea. He knows he is dying.
The swallows come, the twilight falls.
You sleep on the ground. An old man is ill.
Too tired to walk, he wants to die.
Beneath the lovely evening sky
Young Breughel paints the flames of hell.

August 1940

2 Spring

The cries of the boatmen float by on the river,
The warm night stirs like a girl in her sleep,
And the radio sings of such commonplace love
It touches our soldier hearts, and we weep.

A girl dreams on deck beneath the moon
Of the man beside her; a voice in a doorway
As if in a dream, says, 'I'll see you soon,'
Another one mutters, 'They're dying in Norway.'

Fear runs like a canal through strange lands
Beyond the open frontiers of our hearts,
But the sky neither cares nor understands
Where France ends and Belgium starts.

We waited so long for the Winter to pass,
For the violet eyes of May to smile,
For the blood to rise like wine in the glass,
And the Spring to lift its blossoming veil.

We waited so long for the promise of earth,
For the god who must die at the harvest home;
We waited so long for the world to give birth
It's hard to believe that the Spring will still come.

All Winter we hid beneath our kit,
Protected by helmets and gas-masks and orders,
Deaf to the world, the colour of shit,
Keeping watch for the monsters beyond the borders.

We who once slept in a warm lover's bed
Now live estranged from the men we once were,
Loveless and thoughtless and blind, as if dead,
Waiting in vain for the turn of the year.

It's hard to believe that life will return,
That the doors of the season will spring open wide
And love with its perfumed touch will be born
Upskittling the world like the blush of a bride.

But this year, love, the Spring is not ours.
For why should the apple-trees blossom at all?
Without you beside me, my love, nothing flowers
And sweet May is nothing to me but a hell.

My love, my wife, my universe!
Without you the Spring is a desert of grief,
Without you sun is a terrible curse,
Bleached of all colour, all song and belief.

April 1940

3 *Song of the New Barbarism*

Cut off by bombers up ahead
The refugees drift down the roads
As though they are already dead
     The refugees drift down the roads
     The men walk on as if under a spell
     The women bend beneath their loads
The men walk on as if under a spell
The children cry for broken toys
What they have seen they cannot tell
     The children cry for broken toys
     And there's no one who can explain
     The terrifying bomber's noise
And there's no one who can explain
The ruins in the village square
The soldier standing in the lane
     The ruins in the village square
     The soldiers' talk in undertones
     Machine guns on the thoroughfare

The soldiers talk in undertones
They count their wounded and their dead
Inside a school of rubbled stones
    They count their wounded and their dead
    They talk of lovers far away
    Of love, regret, and things unsaid
They talk of lovers far away
The soldiers clutch their photographs
The swallows pick the threads of day
    The soldiers clutch their photographs
    On canvas stretchers in the night
    A line of lovers' epitaphs
On canvas stretchers in the night
We bear the wounded men away
In bandages of red and white
    We bear the wounded men away
    Although it won't do any good
    They'll all be dead within a day
Although it won't do any good
If we can get to Saint-Omer
The tanks are waiting in the wood
    If we can get to Saint-Omer
    We'll never make it to the coast
    The enemy's already there
We'll never make it to the coast
They say they've taken Abbeville
And all is lost and all is lost
    They say they've taken Abbeville
    Like rumours passing through the crowd
    The gunners talk of their ordeal
Like rumours passing through the crowd
Like painted ghosts, so deathly pale
Their eyes are blank, their heads are bowed
    Like painted ghosts, so deathly pale
    And one man when he saw them laughed
    Until he heard their ghostly tale
And one man when he saw them laughed
A hero blackened by the war
A miner coming off his shift

A hero blackened by the war
He's now returning home again
To Sallaumaines or Mericourt
He's now returning home again
Although he's probably going to die
To face the shells that fall like rain
    Although he's probably going to die
    It's better to die in a place you know
    If they're going to kill you from the sky
It's better to die in a place you know
Than to perish alone in a foreign land
These refugees prefer to go
    Than to perish alone in a strange land
    With heavy heart and little hope
    Back to the place they understand
With heavy hearts and little hope
Returning to face the tanks and guns
The refugees cannot escape
    Returning to face the tanks and guns
    Because they've nowhere else to go
    To die beneath the mid-day sun
Because they've nowhere else to go
So many children, husbands, wives
Will die among the fields they know
    So many children, husbands, wives
    This line of refugees crawls back
    Into the flames that claim their lives
This line of refugees crawls back
Civilians who are going to die
Defenceless now against attack
    Civilians who are going to die
    Against the white and angry sky.

August 1940

Yooman

'Here's to you, the army of heavy laden and sweaty bodies. You who are of thirst and fatigue, you who are of industry and not of ambition, inferiors, visited by the fleas . . . the creators of all, the uncouth, the mugs, the seekers of jobs, the possessors of the painful quality of endurance, the dumb and inarticulate, the men of fustian, the cream of the earth . . . general masses, howling mobs, beastly blonds, you are infallible, impeccable, and always right.'
(Jack Hilton, *Caliban Shrieks*)

Yes here's to us and here's to you
And all the Yooman things we do,
The members of a lonely race
On one small planet, lost in space,
The common lot whose common lot
Is knowing that we'll be forgot,
Who do our bit while we are here,
Then suddenly we disappear,
A multitude of nameless proles
Who only get the walk-on roles,
The common folk who know our place
Is here among the Yooman race:

Musicians, florists, lorry drivers,
Astronauts and scuba-divers,
Farmers, cyclists, paperboys,
Small babies who make lots of noise,
The sad, the glad, the barking mad,
The devil-may-care, the Jack-the-lad,
The young, the old, the in-between,
The kind, the blind, the sometimes mean,
Defenders, strikers, centre-backs,
All those who pay their income tax,
Administrators, builders, actors,
Chip-shop owners, girls on tractors,
Bar-maids, chemists, burglars, skaters,
Plumbers, surgeons, shepherds, waiters,

Those who always mow their lawns,
And those who don't like eating prawns,
The overweight, the short, the tall,
And those who think their breasts too small,
The eager, lanky, awkward types,
Thin girls who don't like wearing stripes,
Designers, miners, teenage twockers,
Ramblers, gamblers, jobless dockers,
Boxers into origami,
Boys who want to join the army,
Cornish folk who pick their noses,
Men who cultivate their roses,
Kids who think they're really wired,
And mums and dads who know they're tired,
Trade unionists and referees,
The homeless, homesick refugees,
The men whose wives don't like them snoring,
Wives whose husbands think they're boring,
Smackheads, crackheads, off their faces,
Ageing skins who still wear braces,
Teachers, pupils, dinner-nannies,
Babysitters, anglers, grannies,
Widowers and single mothers,
Older sisters, little brothers,
Those who work in magic shops,
And those who liked *The Woodentops*,
The lazybones, the would-be martyrs,
Businessmen who grow tomatoes,
Optimists who do the lottery,
Big-boned girls who're into pottery,
Loved-up, spaced-out, all-night ravers,
Careless spenders, careful savers,
Slimmers who're obsessed with food,
And poets who don't get reviewed,
Pedestrians and careful drivers,
Jilted lovers, work-shy skivers,
Strippers, trippers, men in bars,
And pensioners who read their stars,
Pubescent boys with nasty habits,
Vicars who like breeding rabbits,

Jokers, smokers, rapid blinkers,
Tinkers, drinkers, heavy thinkers,
Cousins who are good at darts,
Binmen who like Bakewell Tarts,
The hard of hearing, girls who swim,
The pretty and the pretty dim,
Psychologists who sing in choirs,
All those who're good at changing tyres,
The divorcees and newly-weds,
Old men in their allotment sheds,
The don't-know-why and can't-care-less
And those whose lives are in a mess,
The aunties who are always knitting,
Schoolboys who are always spitting,
Diabetics, twitchers, hitchers,
Kids who queue outside the pictures,
Dentists who can't stay awake,
Photographers who don't like cake,
Comedians in Christmas panto,
All those learning Esperanto,
Students who are always late
And teachers who are overweight,
And those who always play the game,
And those who always get the blame,
The down and out, the lost, confused,
And those who think they're being used,
Saxophonists, computer-freaks,
And men who grow prize-winning leeks,
All those who go to Friday prayers
And those who've not stopped wearing flares,
Infertile couples, and the fecund,
Those who always come in second,
Careful drivers, roller-bladers,
Warehouse men and market traders,
Taxi-drivers, wheelchair users,
Girls who think that they are losers,
Plumbers who like playing squash,
Old men who really need a wash,
Thirteen year olds who get embarrassed,
Filing clerks who're don't get harassed,

Chippes, hippies, would-be rogues,
Librarians in polished brogues,
Old couples who like walking dogs
And those who pray in synagogues,
Long-distance runners, pearly queens,
Old men who play on bowling greens,
The careless, hairless, bound to fail,
And those who are banged-up in gaol,
The sentimental and the sly,
The laugh-too-loud, the far-too-shy,
The weak, the cold, the brave and good,
Who try to do the things they should,
And all who stake their little claim
To being Yooman, not to fame;
To all the faces in the crowds
Whose heads are sometimes in the clouds,
Who keep their feet upon the ground,
Who keep this planet spinning round;
To those of us who only count
When added to the whole amount,
Whose worth is not in what we own,
Whose strength's in numbers, not alone,
And all who know themselves to be
No more or less than you or me.

It's not a comprehensive list,
There's lots of Yooman types I've missed;
It isn't easy to describe
The colours of the Yooman tribe,
It's many patterns, shades and stripes
(And these are just some UK types,
There's several billion more elsewhere).
What makes us Yooman's what we share:
The common music which survives
The narratives of common lives.
Being Yooman's easy if you try,
It isn't hard to qualify,
So here's to us, the Yooman race,
Upon this planet, lost in space,
And here's to what this lonely planet
Could be if only Yoomans ran it.

Comrade Laughter Forgets the Punchline

They laughed at us when we declared
It would be really funny
To overthrow the powerful
And end the rule of money.
But now our laughter's spent we're broke
And can't explain to other folk
   the joke.

Comrade Laughter Goes AWOL

There's some say you tore up your card
Fed up with splits and rancour,
There's others saw you at the front,
Or in the Lubyanka,
While others say you're still a Red,
Or is it true, as some have said,
   you're dead?

Notes and Dedications

p.10 Thomas Hardy's 'The Darkling Thrush' was written on 31 December 1900.

p.11 Elizabeth Shaw was an artist and a Communist who settled in the GDR during the Cold War.

p.13 'Dives and Lazarus' attempts to render into modern English the words of an old English folk song; the story of Dives and Lazarus is told in Luke 16, 19.

p.15 Charles Dickens published several stories set in the fictional provincial town of 'Mudfog' (actually the Chatham of his childhood); the radical Teesside journalist William Seymour used the name when writing about late nineteenth-century Middlesbrough; Mudfog is also the name of a small poetry press on Teesside.

p.22 The Celts called the River Tees a land of sunlight and heat.

p.28 'Phrase Book' uses several phrases from an English–German conversation book published in the GDR in the 1970s.

p.29 This poem is a sequel to 'Letter to Randall Swingler', first published as a pamphlet by Shoestring Press in 1999 and subsequently collected in *Just as Blue* (Flambard, 2001). Randall Swingler (1909–67) was an English lyric poet and a Communist; during the Second World War he served with the Eighth Army in Italy, where he was awarded the Military Medal for bravery.

p.39 Ravensbruck, Bursa, Roben Island, Pankrac and Turi were prisons famous for the brutality with which they treated their mostly Communist prisoners.

p.48 Byron's wife Annabella Milbanke came from Hartlepool; the pubs named are to be found on the Hartlepool Headland, past and present.

p.86 'A Tapestry of Modern Terror', 'Spring' and 'Song of the New Barbarism' are versions of poems by Louis Aragon, written after the fall of France in 1940 and published in *Le Crève-Cœur* (1942).

The following poems carry specific dedications: 'Comrade Laughter' is for Charles Hobday, 'Walking on Hampstead Heath with Adrian Mitchell' was written for Adrian Mitchell's seventieth birthday, 'The Neon Thrush' is in memory of Paul Hogarth, 'Dorotheenstädtischer Friedhof' is for Arnold Rattenbury, 'Phrase Book' is for Andrea Kinsky-Ehritt, 'Letter to Randall Swingler Part II' is for Dan Swingler, 'Comrade Laughter: Last Known Whereabouts' is for Chris Searle, 'Alchemical' is for Reuben Kench, 'Crumbs!' and 'On the Re-making of *Goodbye Mr Chips*' are for the staff at King's Manor Comprehensive School in Middlesbrough, 'Included' is for the staff and pupils of The Meadows School in Spennymoor, 'Lost' and 'Too Many Stars to Count' are for Nora Hunter and Heather Peace, 'Yoomans' is in memory of Jack Beeching, 'Comrade Laughter Goes AWOL' is for John Green and Bruni de la Motte.